# JANE AUSTEN'S HOMECOMING
## CHAWTON 1809

*An insight into the life and times of Jane Austen detailing her years at Chawton,
her home and inspiration to many of her famous literary classics.*

*Written by*
*Ben Smith*

JANE AUSTEN'S HOME
GIVEN BY
THOMAS EDWARD CARPENTER, J.P. OF MILL HILL
IN MEMORY OF HIS SON
LIEUT. PHILIP JOHN CARPENTER,
EAST SURREY REGT.
KILLED IN ACTION, LAKE TRASIMENE, 1944
OPENED 1949 BY THE DUKE OF WELLINGTON, K.G.,
PRESIDENT OF THE JANE AUSTEN SOCIETY,
FOUNDED 1940-BY DOROTHY DARNELL, OF ALTON.

*The commemoration plaque on
Jane Austen's House*

"*Those stories*

*Jane Austens house, as it is today in Chawton, Hampshire*

# JANE AUSTEN AT CHAWTON

Jane Austen has become one of the most popular and influential female authors in English literary history. Her novels have been read by generations world-wide, and the film and television adaptations of her romantic stories have been watched by millions. None of this may have been possible if, on 7 July 1809, Jane and her family had not moved into the cottage at Chawton. This seemingly insignificant event was to herald the birth of the modern English novel. It was here, in this quiet and secluded part of the Hampshire countryside that Jane found the inner peace and security that she needed to write and revise her stories. Those stories have so grasped the essence of the period, and the characters have almost stepped off the pages to take on a life of their own, so that her books have rarely been out of print for nearly two centuries.

# JANE, WHO IS SHE?

Who was this young woman who came to this little village to write her stories? Where did she find her inspiration for her characters and her richly veined story lines?

Jane Austen's life has been chronicled in far more detail than we have time for here, and several excellent biographies of her are available. But to get a feel for Jane and the way her life experiences influenced her writing whilst she was here, we need to look at her family background. Despite the fact that Jane wrote so much about her family and friends in her life, she wrote very little about herself. In fact all that is known about Jane has been pieced together from letters and journals kept by her siblings and cousins.

Jane grew up in a close-knit and loving family, the second daughter and seventh child in a family of eight. Her father, the Revd George Austen, was rector of the two parishes of Steventon and Deane in north-east Hampshire. The Austens were a long-established family of farming yeomen throughout Kent who had grown wealthy through the booming wool trade. Sadly George's branch of the family had not acquired much in the way of wealth and he was orphaned early in life. His upbringing and subsequent education was provided by his wealthy uncle Francis, a successful solicitor in Sevenoaks, Kent. Through his patronage George was able to study at St John's College, Oxford, and to go on to take holy orders. It was at Oxford that he was first introduced to his wife, Miss Cassandra Leigh, the daughter of the Revd Thomas Leigh, the rector of Harpsden in Oxfordshire. They were married in Walcot church in Bath on 26 April 1764. George was a tall, slim, handsome man with a bright mind and a thirst for knowledge. By all accounts he was a good scholar and enjoyed his time at university. He was by nature a gentle man who was devoted to his family and cared deeply for his

parishioners. Mrs Austen was a petite, slim woman with dark hair, grey eyes and what one could only describe as an 'aristocratic' nose. She was the perfect partner for a country parson: bright and quick-witted with a sparkling personality; always busy organising her household and large family. Jane inherited all of her parents' qualities, which would serve her well throughout her life and in her writing.

*Mrs Austen*

# THE EARLY DAYS

Life as a country parson in those days was, without the resources of a wealthy family, challenging to say the least. Revd Austen supplemented his modest stipend by farming and tutoring three or four boys at a time, who boarded with the family. Despite the lack of funds, life in the Austen household was lived in an open, amused and easy intellectual atmosphere. Jane's father had a passion for books and during his life built up a library of over 500 volumes of subjects as diverse as literary classics of the time, science, physics and philosophy. He willingly gave his children, and unusually for the time his daughters, unrestricted access to this varied library. Although Jane and her sister Cassandra spent a short period at boarding school, they gained a wider and far more enlightened education at home from the tuition of their father and elder brothers. Jane's brothers and cousins would often get together and arrange theatrical productions for the Christmas holidays under the enthusiastic direction of James, the eldest. Although Jane was too young to play anything other than minor parts, she was an eager participant and was caught up in the excitement and preparations. These memories would later become woven into her novels. It was in this atmosphere that Jane's imagination grew and where her writing skills were developed through short stories and comic parodies written for the amusement and entertainment of her family. These were to become known collectively as her 'Juvenilia' and written between 1787 and 1793.

## THE MOVE TO BATH

Why was the move to Chawton such an important event in Jane's life? To understand this we need to look back a few years. By 1800 Jane was 25 and had written three, as yet unpublished, novels and she seemed set on a path as an author, which was no mean feat for a woman at that time. Instead she fell silent for nearly ten years.

It was around Jane's 25th birthday that Revd Austen announced to his family that he intended to retire to Bath, where the family could enjoy the society of the big city.

*Mr Austen*

This was a shock to all the family as it had not been discussed openly with any of them. Steventon had been the family home for over 30 years. Jane's brother James would be installed as curate to his father, thereby allowing him to retire with an income from the 'living' at Steventon. Life at Steventon had been hard work for Jane's father, now nearly seventy; he had supplemented his income with farming and teaching, and whilst he had managed to support his family and educate his children, they had accumulated little in the way of wealth.

Now that his sons had left home to forge their own lives, there would be less strain on his resources to support a smaller family. The need to 'downsize', as we would call it today, meant that most of the Revd Austen's extensive library of 500 books would have to be sold, along with most of the furniture and even the piano on which Jane learned, practised and played, and a large collection of sheet music. It must have been hard for Jane to see the familiar parts of her childhood and now her adult life sold off to the highest bidder, and she felt more than a little resentment towards her sister-in-law Mary, James' wife, whom she saw taking to the role of 'mistress of the house' with more that a little relish. Jane was caught up in a situation over which she had no control, losing the life she loved in the country for one in the city, and faced with a future full of uncertainty.

Mrs Austen firmly believed that the move to Bath would be good for her health and that of her husband. She would also be closer to her rich, friendly and hospitable brother James Leigh-Perrot. There was also that fact that both were approaching their seventies with two unmarried daughters in their late twenties. The prospects for either of them finding suitable husbands would be greatly enhanced by a move to the city. Mr Austen also extolled the virtues of their new location as being close to Wales and Devon, where they could venture for holidays; neither of these opportunities seemed to appeal to Jane, however.

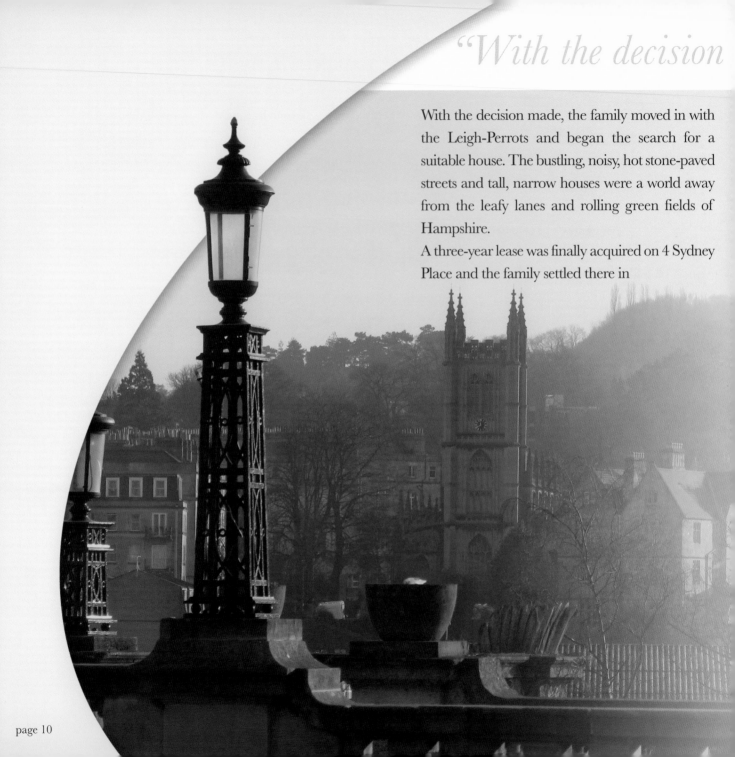

With the decision made, the family moved in with the Leigh-Perrots and began the search for a suitable house. The bustling, noisy, hot stone-paved streets and tall, narrow houses were a world away from the leafy lanes and rolling green fields of Hampshire.

A three-year lease was finally acquired on 4 Sydney Place and the family settled there in

October 1801. Jane seemed reconciled, for the moment at least, to the thought of a new life in Bath society, and set about with her mother and sister making the home as comfortable as possible.

Although they had now taken up residence in the city, the Austens travelled extensively throughout the West Country and the south coast. Summer holidays were taken in Dawlish, Teignmouth and along the Dorset coast in Lyme Regis. They also spent time visiting friends and relatives in Kent. For us living in the 21st century, travel is a relatively simple thing to arrange; with a network of motorways and rail links we can get from one end of the country to another in a day. Two hundred years ago travelling even a short distance was not without its problems, and needed plenty of preparation and planning, not to mention the slow progress of horse-drawn vehicles on very primitive roads. When you did arrive it was usually for a stay of several weeks to make the journey worth while. All of this travelling and visiting relatives and friends gave Jane very little opportunity to settle to her writing. As a consequence, her creative output declined rapidly. Although she kept her manuscripts by her, she would find only a few hours here and there in which to do some revision and redrafting.

She did succeed in selling the manuscript of Susan (Northanger Abbey) to Richard Crosby, a London publisher, for the sum of £10 in 1803. However he changed his mind and it was never published. Jane began work on a new novel but seemed to abandon the work after the death of her farther.

When the lease on Sydney Place expired the family moved closer to the centre of Bath, to 3 Green Park Buildings, another upheaval for Jane. Yet again she received some disturbing news, on her 29th birthday, about the death of her close childhood friend Madame Lefroy, killed in an accident caused by a bolting horse. Within another month Jane had to cope with the death of her dear father on 21 January after only two days' illness. This was possibly one of the lowest points in Jane's life.

The Revd George Austen (1731-1805), Rector of Steventon in Hampshire, married Cassandra Leigh (1739-1827) at the medieval church of St. Swithin's Walcot, on 26 April 1764.

Their seventh child was the novelist Jane Austen (1775-1817), author of *Sense and Sensibility, Pride and Prejudice, Mansfield Park, Emma, Northanger Abbey and Persuasion.*

With her parents and sister Cassandra, Jane Austen came to live in Bath in 1801, at 4 Sydney Place until 1804, and then at 3 Green Park Buildings East, where George Austen died on 21 January 1805. He was buried in the crypt of the rebuilt (1779-90) church of St Swithin's.

His tombstone was removed to the present site in 1968. In 2000 it was remounted and this plaque erected by the Jane Austen Society, with help from the Bath and Bristol branch and the Jane Austen Societies of North America and of Australia.

unable to write. But despite moving so often, and disposing of all their furniture, she always carried with her the manuscripts of three unpublished novels, Elinor and Marianne, First Impressions, and Susan.

Jane and her mother eventually took lodgings in Southampton while they looked around for a suitable house to rent. Jane was recovering from a bout of whooping-cough, which she had caught on a recent visit to a cousin in Staffordshire, and her first few months here were far from happy. By this time the Austen ladies had been joined permanently by Martha Lloyd, who became almost a third daughter to Mrs Austen and a companion to Jane and Cassandra. Jane's brother Frank and his wife Mary came to Southampton and took a lease on 'a commodious old-fashioned house in a corner of Castle Square'. The house had a large garden bounded on one side by the old city wall that was washed by the tides of Southampton Water. There were extensive views across to the wooded slopes of the Isle of Wight and pleasant walks for the ladies to enjoy.

*A lock of Jane's Father's hair*

After her father died, Jane had moved twice more with her mother and her sister, each time to lodgings less expensive than the last. There was no provision for pensions in the clergy and the Austen ladies found themselves in greatly reduced circumstances, relying on the good will and support of family and friends. It was not a happy time, and Jane wrote that they left Bath with 'what happy feelings of Escape!'

Next they stayed in Clifton, and with relatives at Adlestrop, at Stoneleigh, and in Kent. During this very unsettled period, Jane Austen seemed

christening of his daughter in May and stayed until June, when he sailed for the Cape. It was during their time in Southampton that Jane and her mother first saw Chawton.

Edward had come over to see the family in Southampton and suggested that they should join him at Chawton House in September for a family holiday. Although the grandeur of the house impressed the ladies, it was the attraction of the shops at Alton the seemed to give Jane thegreatest pleasure, where her niece, Fanny, recorded three shopping trips with her aunt Jane in five days.

They returned to their life in Southampton, and for the next year Jane's time was split between her brothers families. If she was not with Francis, Mary and their baby in Southampton, she was tending to Edward's ten children at Godmersham, or with James and his three at Steventon. It seemed that Jane was to become the maiden aunt that everyone could rely on to help. There was scarcely a place, or time that Jane could call her own; the demands of her sisters-in-law and their pregnancies, along with

# SOUTHAMPTON

Jane's health improved as did her mood, and she spent many pleasant hours helping her mother plan the garden, and was kept busy supervising the cleaning and furnishing of the house. They eventually moved in during early March 1807. After settling his family and ensuring that his wife was in the loving care of his mother and sisters, Frank received news that he had been given command of a new ship , the St Albans, and had to leave to supervise its fitting out ready for convoy duty to the Cape of Good Hope. However he did get home in time for the their broods of children seemed to take over Jane's life and her writing dwindled away to nothing. In August of 1808, Frank returned home to announce that he and Mary wanted to move to a home of their own on the Isle of Wight. Once more Jane, Cassandra and their mother had to face the prospect of an uncertain future as far as a home was concerned.

*Charles Austen*

*Francis Austen*

*Jane Austen's house as it is today*

## THE MOVE TO CHAWTON

It was Jane's older brother Edward who was to prove to be the benefactor to his mother and sisters. Edward had been formally adopted by a wealthy cousin of the Revd Austen, Thomas Knight II. Thomas married Catherine Knatchbull and set up home in Godmersham, near Canterbury. Despite great wealth and a happy and loving marriage, they were childless.

It was not uncommon in those days for distant branches of families to adopt a child to give them a better start in life, even though both parents were still alive. Both Thomas and Catherine were captivated by Edward, then aged 12, and proposed that they would like to adopt him. It was an arrangement that seemed to be agreeable to all parties, and Edward was to spend his time studying under his father's tuition and spending his holidays with his newly acquired family. And so in 1783 Edward was formally adopted into the Knight family and became heir to a substantial fortune and large estates in Kent and Hampshire.

By 1807 Edward had inherited the estates and had a substantial family of 11 children. Sadly, after giving birth to her last baby, Elizabeth Austen died suddenly two weeks later. It seemed that his bereavement brought Edward closer to his mother and sisters. He made them the offer of a choice of houses on either the Godmersham estate, close to his own home, or the Chawton estate. Mrs Austen was most grateful for his generosity and, as they had fond memories of their visit to Chawton, it seemed to be the most prudent choice.

Jane often referred to the former farm bailiff's house on the Chawton estate as 'the cottage', despite its having six bedrooms, servants, quarters and a large garden. The house had a colourful past, having once been the 'New Inn', a coaching or posting inn around 1769, due to its location where the road from London branches; one route goes south to Gosport, and the other west to Winchester. It was a lively, busy place offering a welcome break to travellers on a tedious and uncomfortable journey. The inn remained in business for only 18 years, as the good parishioners of Chawton had a long aversion to pubs and felt that the hospitality on offer at the 'New Inn' was being enjoyed a little too much by the locals, and was proving to be more trouble than it was worth.

*Jane Austen's house as it was*

The closure of the inn did nothing to reduce the volume of traffic on the road. Today there is a by-pass, but the road was busy when Jane and her family moved in. A turnpike built in 1753 made travel easy. The large coaches with six horses were quite a sight as they passed through the village every day from Alton. There were two coaches a day from Winchester and one at mid-day from Portsmouth. From the cottage the Austens watched people pass by. Jane wrote to her nephew one day how they had seen 'a countless number of Postchaises full of Boys pass by full of future Heroes, Legislators, Fools and Villains' going to school in Winchester.

The move to Chawton, which is today naturally regarded as Jane's literary home, at last gave her the peace and stability that had been so lacking in the past years. Here was somewhere she could settle with her family, back in her beloved Hampshire countryside, without the worry and uncertainty that she had gone through after her father's death. She again took up her pen at a little table by the parlour window and resumed novel-writing with a new-found passion. It was here that she revised both Sense & Sensibility, which was published in 1811 (and made Jane £140), and Pride & Prejudice, which was published in 1813.

## LIFE IN CHAWTON

This was an instant success. All Jane's novels that appeared during her lifetime were published anonymously, merely bearing the legend 'By a Lady', which was not uncommon at the time. Mansfield Park was published in 1814 and Emma in 1815. Persuasion was completed in 1816 but was not published until 1818, after Jane's death in 1817. Northanger Abbey was also published in 1818.

The Austen ladies, in the company of Martha Lloyd, a close friend and confidante of Jane for many years, settled into their new home. It is clear from Jane's correspondence that her friend Martha was privy to her great secret - her writing - an honour accorded to few.

Jane was so taken with Chawton that she wrote to her brother James:

*Our Chawton home, how much we find*

*Already in it to our mind;*

*And how convinced that when complete*

*It will all other houses beat*

*That ever have been made or mended,*

*With rooms concise or rooms*

*distended*

*Martha Lloyd*

# DOMESTIC DUTIES

The ladies had developed a domestic regime that suited all of them comfortably. Mrs Austen had taken on the task of looking after and maintaining the garden, keeping the flower beds and shrubbery in order and growing vegetables for the kitchen. Martha took on the responsibility of arranging all the meals of the day save breakfast; that task fell to Jane. She would rise early and often practise at the piano or write a little before preparing tea and toast for the rest of the family. Once her duties had been discharged, she was free to spend the rest of the day at her small table writing, whilst Cassandra and Martha supervised the rest of the housekeeping. It has to be said that a great deal of Jane's success has to be credited to the love, devotion and support that she received from Cassandra. It was she who recognised the talent in her sister and gave her the encouragement and freedom to develop her writing.

The house as it is now has changed very little. The rooms on show include the drawing room, and the parlour where Jane wrote on the small round table. Upstairs is her bedroom with a handmade bowed canopy tent bed of the type Jane might have had while living here. There are four other rooms, one of which has memorabilia of her two brothers, Frank and Charles, who both had distinguished careers in the Royal Navy. Another room houses the patchwork quilt Jane made with her mother and sister.

There is an extensive collection of family mementoes and documentary material, including copies of letters written by her.

A pretty garden surrounds the house, stocked with many old varieties of flowers and herbs, and Jane's donkey carriage is displayed in the adjoining old bakehouse.

# JANE AUSTEN'S HOUSE MUSEUM

Over the years it is often the large and robust items in our lives that survive. Often the small, personal items that we acquire are either discarded or lost. But here at Chawton some of Jane's most intimate, personal items are on display.

# DAILY LIFE AT CHAWTON

And so life took on a much more measured and idyllic pace for Jane and her family. Jane and Cassandra normally went for a walk every day and used to go shopping in Alton, where their brother Henry, who was a London banker, had a branch bank. This was at 10 High Street, where the family post was delivered and collected.

Also near Alton, and within walking distance of Chawton, was Wyards, the home of Anna and Ben Lefroy. Anna was the eldest daughter of Jane's brother, James, from his first marriage to Anne Mathew. Jane and Cassandra were very fond of their niece, often visiting her or having her to stay with them in Chawton, and her memories recorded in later years provide a lot of biographical information about Jane.

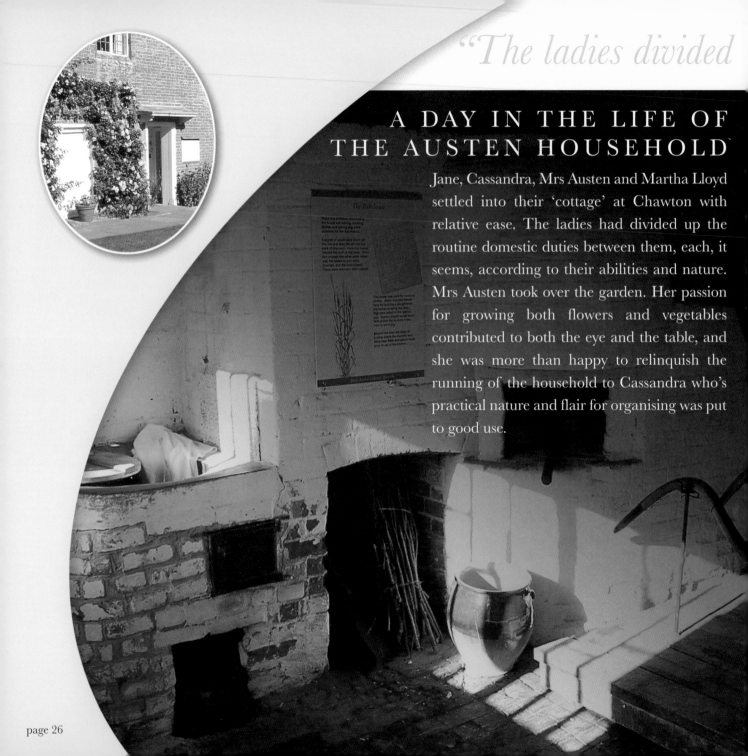

# A DAY IN THE LIFE OF THE AUSTEN HOUSEHOLD

Jane, Cassandra, Mrs Austen and Martha Lloyd settled into their 'cottage' at Chawton with relative ease. The ladies had divided up the routine domestic duties between them, each, it seems, according to their abilities and nature. Mrs Austen took over the garden. Her passion for growing both flowers and vegetables contributed to both the eye and the table, and she was more than happy to relinquish the running of the household to Cassandra who's practical nature and flair for organising was put to good use.

Mrs Austen, now in her seventies, took to her gardening with passion and enthusiasm, digging her own potatoes and wearing a green round frock like a day-labourer, much to the amusement of the locals. During the summer months the garden was a riot of colour with sweet Williams, columbines, peonies, pinks and laburnums. They also had an orchard for greengages, plums and a range of soft fruits such as raspberries, gooseberries and currants which kept the larder well-stocked with jams and preserves through the winter months. The ladies also kept chickens, a pig and had a small field for their two donkeys. And just to add a little sweetness to the pot, Cassandra kept bees.

Martha Lloyd had, by this time, had become a permanent member of the household. The Lloyd family had much in common with the Austens and from an early time, visits between the two families were frequent. Though no one knows quite how they met, the Austens and Lloyds shared many mutual friends and when the Rev. Lloyd died in 1789, his widow and her two oldest, single daughters were happy to move into

the unused Deane parsonage offered by Rev. Austen. Their time there, only a mile and a half from Steventon, must have been a delight for young Jane, for though she was ten years younger than the oldest Lloyd daughter, Martha, they were, as Janes' cousin Eliza de Feuillide remarked, 'very sensible and good-humored.' Martha was an excellent cook and, although they employed a cook at Chawton, it was Martha who supervised the meals and also created a cook book that still survives today. (Martha was later to become an Austen as she married Jane's widowed brother, then Admiral Sir Francis Austen, in 1828.)

> A Prayer by Jane Austen
>
> Give us grace almighty Father, so to pray as to deserve to be heard, to address thee with our hearts, as with our lips. Thou art everywhere present, from thee no secret can be hid. May the knowledge of this, teach us to fix our thoughts on thee, with reverence and devotion that we pray not in vain. ~
>
> May we now, and on each return of night, consider how the past day has been spent by us, what have been our prevailing thoughts, words and actions during it, and how far we can acquit ourselves of evil. ~
>
> Have we thought irreverently of thee, have we disobeyed thy commandments, have we neglected any known duty, or willingly given pain to any human being? Incline us to ask our hearts these questions Oh! God, to save us from deceiving ourselves by pride or vanity ~
>
> Give us a thankful sense of the blessings in which we live, of the many comforts of our lot; that we may not deserve to lose them by discontent or indifference ~ Hear us almighty God, for his sake who has redeemed us, and taught us, thus to pray ~
>
> Amen.

## JANE'S CREATIVITY

This left Jane with very little in the way of responsibilities other than the preparation of the family breakfast at nine o'clock consisting of tea and toast, both made on the dining room fire. Jane was always the first to rise, and while the maid laid the fire and filled the kettle, Jane would practise at the piano which stood in the drawing room far enough away as not to wake the rest of the family, or she would sit and think about her plots and characters. Jane's only other household responsibility was as the keeper of the key to the wine cupboard. Cassandra realised that Jane's creativity needed an opportunity to flourish, and by relieving her of domestic chores it allowed Jane time to sit and write her wonderful stories.

Chawton was a happy house, often frequented by James's three children – Anna, James Edward and Caroline, who came from Steventon to spend time with their grandmother and aunts. Jane was adored by her nieces and nephews, because she had such a sweet charm and easy manner with the children; always finding endless ways of amusing and entertaining them, often with her impromptu stories of Fairyland where each fairy had a character all of its own, and aunt Jane would spin the story out for days on end to keep the children amused.

*needed an opportunity to flourish"*

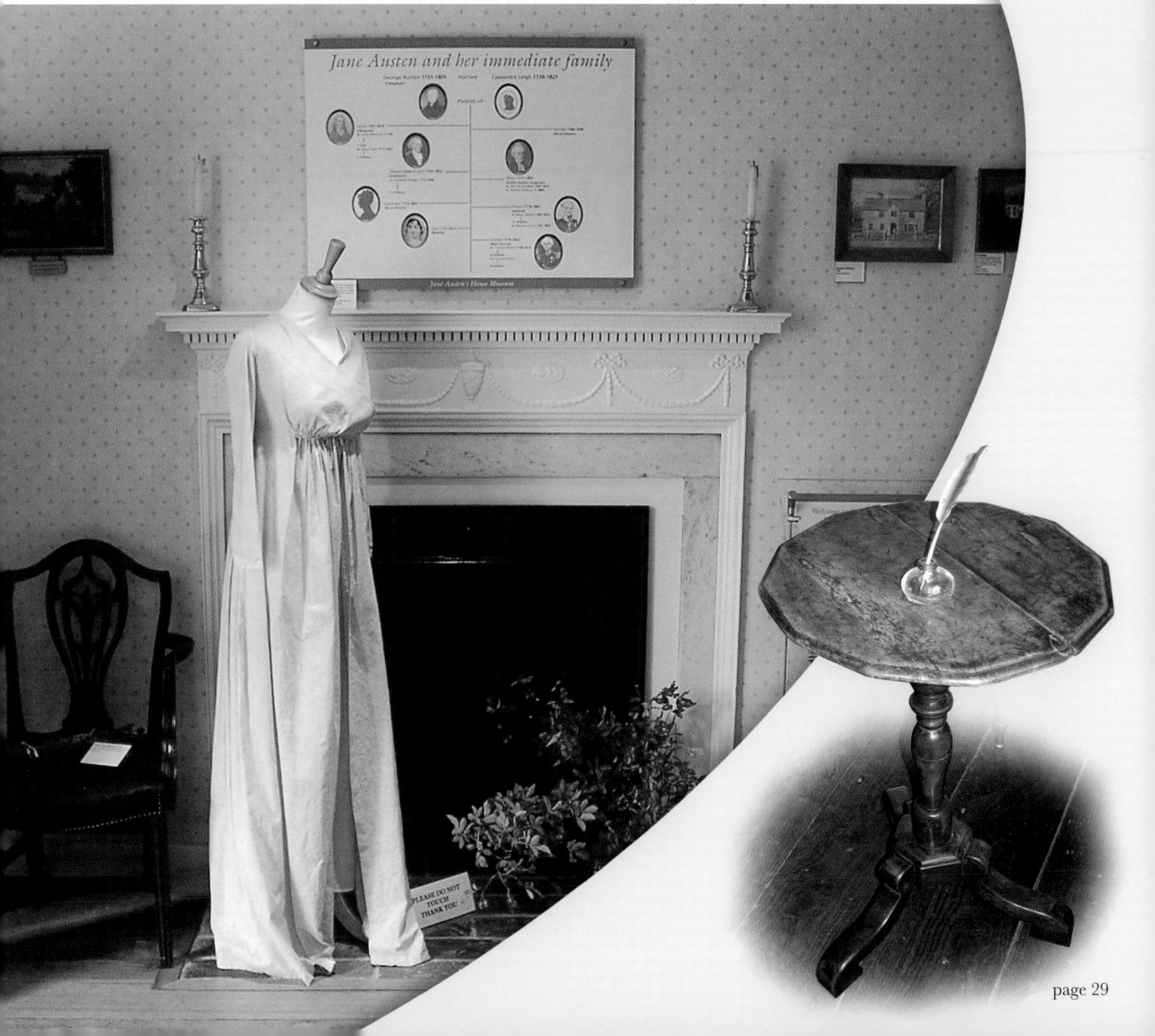

## THE AUSTEN LADIES

The Austen ladies did not enter into the social life in Chawton, dinners and dances were not as abundant as they had been in Steventon, but they were not aloof from the village, and would always be on hand to help out a neighbour. They were also invited to visit relatives and friends in Alton for afternoon tea and the occasional dinner, and they would visit Chawton House when relatives were living there.

The ladies would pass their time at their allotted tasks, and in the late afternoon and evenings would engage in some knitting, patchwork or embroidery. Jane would often entertain the family by reading short extracts from her stories, or play games with her visiting nephews and nieces.

## SHOPPING AT ALTON

A real treat was a shopping trip to Alton. Quite an event that required some planning, as travelling even relatively short distances in those days could be fraught with problems, not to mention being at the mercy of the weather. Edward had provided his mother with a donkey-cart – which would be the equivalent to a very small car by today's standards. It gave them the opportunity to visit brother Henry's bank where they could send their letters to him in London through the bank's internal mail. Compared to Chawton, Alton was a busy, bustling little town that was full of interesting shops and lively, colourful characters. Jane would go about her business, but always found time to just stop and watch, noting the fashions and catching snippets of conversations and overheard gossip. This was how she created the texture and the colour of her characters. Her keen eyes and ears drinking in every drop of this wonderful mixture of town life, later to be distilled and refined in her stories.

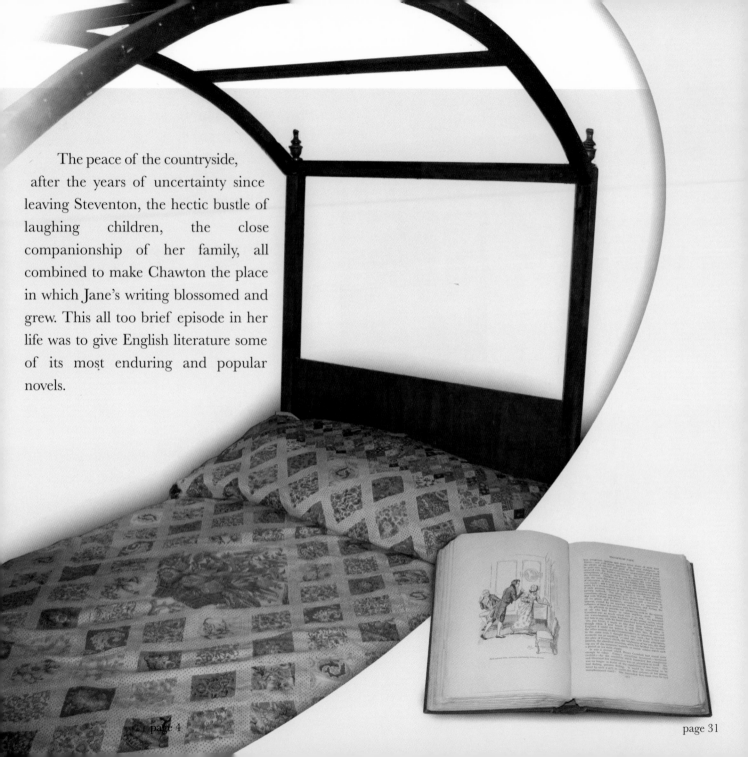

The peace of the countryside, after the years of uncertainty since leaving Steventon, the hectic bustle of laughing children, the close companionship of her family, all combined to make Chawton the place in which Jane's writing blossomed and grew. This all too brief episode in her life was to give English literature some of its most enduring and popular novels.

world-wide favourite for 200 years. Today, Chawton is a place that is visited by Jane's admirers from all over the world. However, the former Austen house is not the only attraction of this quiet little village. Physically, the village has barely changed since Jane's day. Both Jane and Cassandra wrote about the village and their neighbours in their letters, and with information from other local sources, the Chawton of Jane Austen can still be imagined.

It is fair to say that the village was typical for its day, being part of the rural pattern of English life in the Regency period. Life here was governed, even until relatively recently, by the 'lord of the manor', or 'squire', from Chawton's splendid 'Great House'. Usually the largest land-owner in the district, he would be involved in all aspects of village life, and had a controlling influence on the nearby parish church. For example, until the outbreak of the Second World War, the 'squire' ensured that a curfew bell was rung every evening at 8 p.m. (33 tolls, plus the day and the month), for the benefit of his tenants without the advantage of a watch or calendar.

## CHAWTON VILLAGE

If Jane Austen were to return to Chawton today would she recognise it as the place that she left all those years ago? Her happy, secure home at the junction of two busy roads, where she would observe the passengers in the coaches passing by her window, while she sat at the tiny table in her parlour writing and revising her novels.

Jane would probably be both amazed and gratified at her popularity. It is incredible that the work of a young spinster, hardly recognised in her own lifetime, could have such a profound effect on English literature, and become a

In Jane's time, the whole of the manor of Chawton had been made over to Jane's third brother, Edward, in 1797, a substantial inheritance which had included property elsewhere in Hampshire (including their birthplace at Steventon) and at Godmersham in Kent.

These estates were made over to Edward Austen by the widowed Mrs Thomas Knight. The Knights were distant relatives of the Austens and were sadly childless. They had taken a great liking to young Edward and had begun treat him as their adopted son. He would go to stay with them during the summer holidays, and when he grew to be a young man, they sent him on the 'Grand Tour' of Europe to complete his education and prepare him for society. Eventually they appointed him the sole heir to both their name and their property.

Thomas Knight's father, a Brodnax of Godmersham, had himself inherited Chawton from a cousin, Elizabeth Knight (formerly Martin). Whenever she paid a visit here the occasion used to be celebrated with a peal of bells, to let the whole village know of her arrival. Elizabeth had been the nearest surviving relative and heiress of Sir Richard Knight, last of the Knights of Chawton, who had died in 1679.

No manor could be considered complete without its 'Great House' to give the 'squire' his seat of power and, to all intents and purposes, it became the centre of local social and economic activity. Chawton House - the 'Great House' - is at the southern end of the village, on a hillside above the church.

It is now the Chawton House Library, a charitable trust, with a unique collection of books focusing on women's writing in English from 1600 to 1830. This specialist collection provides the opportunity for students and academics from around the world to study and savour the texts in their original setting and inspires passion in readers of all ages, and to protect and preserve Chawton House, as an excellent example of a typical English manor house dating from the Elizabethan period.

It is sometimes open for guided tours but not to the general public, but the west front can be viewed from the gate. Both the house and the church are reached by the carriage-drive, which connects them to the old Gosport Road.

# THE VILLAGE CENTRE

The village centre consists of a cluster of buildings where the grand villas of the gentry rub shoulders with the tiny, cramped cottages of local farm labourers and artisans. Although today the interiors have been modernised, some of the buildings still retain the thatched roofs and stand proud, though now showing their age, yet still conjuring up the image of a typical

English rural scene. The local pub, school and a cricket pitch complete the picture, and in the summer, the sound of the snap of cricket ball being hit for six and the cheers from the team provides the sound-track. Surprisingly little in the way of our modern 'improvements' have made it unrecognisable to Jane. Maybe, if she were to take a stroll through her beloved Chawton today she would still feel at home and as at peace as she did all those years ago.

## THE BROTHERS AUSTEN

Jane had six brothers and they all had a strong influence on her life and work. They encouraged her to develop her personality and her literary skills, involving her from an early age in the 'family entertainments' that they wrote and produced at the parsonage at Steventon. Throughout her life, Jane remained close to them.

### James – 1765 – 1819

The eldest of the family and often thought to be the 'literary one', James followed his father by attending Oxford University at the age of 14 in 1779. Together with his brother Henry they edited a university magazine called The Loiterer, which ran for 60 issues. He was ordained in 1787 at the age of 22 and after his marriage, he became his father's curate at Deane, and after his retirement, he took on the duties of the Steventon parish as well.

James was not Jane Austen's favourites brother, though she did call him 'good and clever'. James was not an outwardly cheerful man: he had an air of melancholy about him which was uncharacteristic of the other Austens. His demeanour could be a result of leaving the intellectual and social excitement of Oxford for the retired life of a country vicar, or maybe seeing his literary ambitions lived out through his sister or the wealth acceded to by his younger brother. It is true that his life was not untouched by sorrow, as well. His first wife died when their daughter, Anna (1793-1872), was but two years old. Anna was the first niece and a favourite of

Jane Austen. She also had her father's creative streak and worked on a novel, Which is the Heroine?, with the help of her aunt, until Jane Austen's death, at which time Anna burned the work.

James married again and his second wife, Mary Lloyd, was not a favourite of Jane Austen, even though she was the sister of her dear friend, Martha Lloyd. James and Mary had two children, James Edward (1798-1874) and Caroline (1805-1880), who also solicited their aunt's approval of their literary efforts. Caroline later wrote down her memories of her Aunt Jane.

## George - 1766-1838

It could be said that George was the 'family secret' as not much is known about him. Though he lived a relatively long life, characteristic of his mother's side of the family, he spent the whole of it living with a farming family a few miles from Steventon. There has been speculation that he was mentally retarded, others have thought that he was merely deaf, owing to Jane Austen's comment that she was

fluent in 'finger speaking'. Whatever the cause of his exile from the family, George was destined to play little part in the Austens' daily lives.

## Edward Knight - 1767-1852

Edward was the only Austen brother not to have a profession. Early in the 1780s he was adopted by Mr Austen's Patron, the rich but childless Thomas and Catherine Knight. Instead of going off to university, like his father and brothers before him, Edward was sent on the 'grand tour' of continental Europe in 1786-1788, as befitted a young gentleman of wealth and position. He eventually inherited their

16 when her mother died. She was another favourite niece who looked to her Aunt Jane for emotional as well as literary guidance. Unfortunately, Jane Austen died before she saw her niece find her own true love. Fanny eventually married a baronet; her son edited the first edition of Jane Austen's letters.

### Henry Thomas - 1771-1850

Henry was Jane Austen's favourite brother and he was most like her in looks and temperament. Witty, amusing and enthusiastic in everything he did, he was the eternal optimist. Henry was 'a glass half full' person. He entered Oxford in 1788 in time to co-edit The Loiterer with his brother James. He and James also shared a passion for the same woman, their widowed cousin, Eliza de Feuillide. She eventually chose Henry, 10 years her junior, and they were married in 1797.

Thanks in part to Eliza's influence, Henry chose not to join James in the ministry, although the family had expected him to follow his brother, and instead chose the militia. He later tried banking and lived the life of a London business

estate of Godmersham, Kent, and took the last name of 'Knight'. As part of his inheritance, Edward also acquired Steventon and an estate in Chawton.

Edward had a large family and a lively, cultured wife, Elizabeth whom, he adored. Cassandra and Jane were frequent visitors to Godmersham during the early years, and when Elizabeth died during her eleventh confinement Aunt Cassandra and Aunt Jane became an integral part of the Godmersham, and then Chawton, life.

Edward's oldest daughter, Fanny, had just turned

man until the bank failed, owing to economic factors, in 1815. His wife, Eliza, had died two years previously and Henry turned back to the Church, eventually becoming a Calvinist-leaning minister. He served at different times in the curacy of Steventon and Chawton before becoming the Perpetual Curate at Bentley.

It was Henry who was most influential in helping Jane Austen to publish her works. Not only was his home available for her to stay in during her trips to London to work with her publisher, but these visits also gave her an insight into society life. It was Henry who saw to the publication of Persuasion and Northanger Abbey after her death, and he who wrote the loving biographical piece which prefaced these two novels. He provided the world with their first tantalising glimpse into the life of his beloved sister Jane.

## Francis William - 1774–1865

Francis Austen served in the Navy from the age of 12 and had the most 'glittering' career of the Austen brothers, eventually achieving a knighthood as Sir Francis Austen and rising to the rank of Admiral of the Fleet. Francis was recognised by none other than Admiral Nelson as 'an excellent young man'.

Could it have been the stories of her dashing brothers that gave Jane such an admiration for the men of the Royal Navy? Francis could have been not only the inspiration for the young Lieutenant William Price in Mansfield Park, but even more so for the unforgettable Captain Wentworth of Persuasion.

Francis and his wife, Mary, had a close, warm relationship with the Austen ladies, even including them for some time in their household in Southampton from 1805 to 1808, after the death of Rev. Austen. This arrangement suited them all,

of his brother, he rose to become a Rear-Admiral. He was stationed in the West Indies, much to the regret of his family, for seven years without once taking leave to visit home, returning at the end of that time with a wife and child. It was Charles' gift of Topaz crosses to his sisters that inspired a similar scene in Mansfield Park. Charles Austen's ship, *Endymion*, was responsible for capturing many prizes during the war with France, leaving him with a comfortable income. He died, at age 73, still on active duty, during a naval river-war in Burma.

as Frank was often at sea, and it also included their close friend, Martha Lloyd, sister to James Austen's wife Mary.

### Charles John - 1779-1852

Last but by no means least was Charles, Jane's particular, little brother, who was a favourite with both sisters as a boy. Following in Francis' footsteps, he also joined the Naval Academy as Midshipman at the age of 12. Although his career was nowhere near as distinguished as that

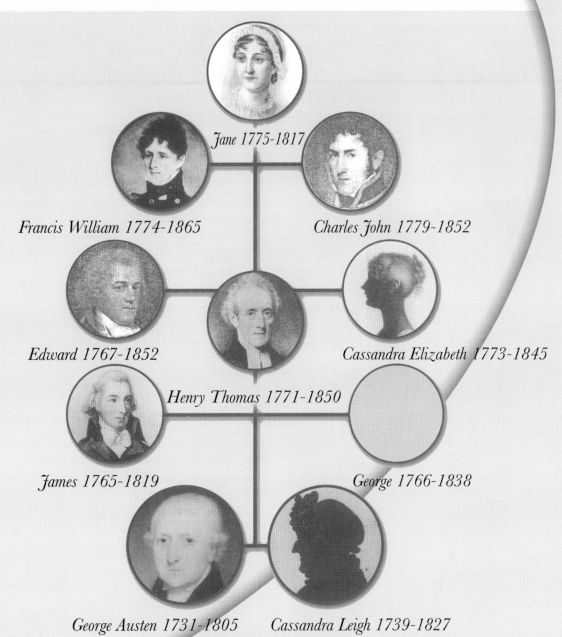

Jane 1775-1817

Francis William 1774-1865

Charles John 1779-1852

Edward 1767-1852

Cassandra Elizabeth 1773-1845

Henry Thomas 1771-1850

James 1765-1819

George 1766-1838

George Austen 1731-1805

Cassandra Leigh 1739-1827

# ACKNOWLEDGEMENTS

*The author and publisher wish to gratefully acknowledge the support*
*and cooperation of the following people:*

Ann Channon & Louise West
Jane Austen's House Museum, Chawton, Alton, Hampshire. GU34 1SD
www.jane-austens-house-museum.org.uk

Costume photographs: Tanya Elliot
Photography: Duncan Allison, Stuart Short, Ben Smith & Peter Wright
Editor: Vernon Mason
Director of design & artwork: Stuart Short of Shorts Associates

### Further reading:

*The Essential Guide to Finding Jane Austen in Chawton*
*By Elizabeth Proudman*

*Chawton: Jane Austen's Village*
*By Rupert Willoughby*

*Jane Austen - A Life*
*By Claire Tomalin*

*The British Library Writers' Lives Series*
*Jane Austen*
*By Deirdre Le Faye*

Published by Trail Publishing
Copyright Trail Publishing
Series Director: Duncan Allison